guardrails

avoiding regrets in your life

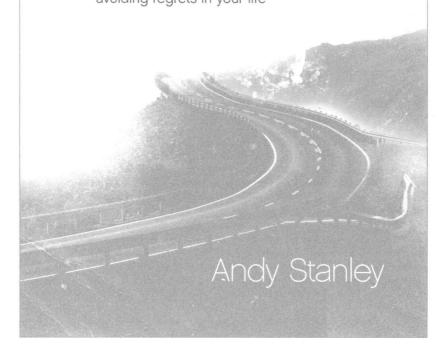

Andy Stanley

 ZONDERVAN®

NORTH POINT RESOURCES

ZONDERVAN.com/
AUTHORTRACKER
follow your favorite authors

ZONDERVAN

Guardrails Participant's Guide
Copyright © 2011 by North Point Ministries, Inc.

Requests for information should be addressed to:
Zondervan, *Grand Rapids, Michigan 49530*

ISBN 978-0-310-89399-8

Cover and interior design: Brian Manley (funwithrobots.com)

Printed in the United States of America

11 12 13 14 15 16 /DCI/ 20 19 18 17 16 15 14 13 12 11 10 9 8 7 6 5 4 3

CONTENTS

INTRODUCTION

Design Your System

by Andy Stanley

Everybody knows what guardrails are. But you probably don't know the official definition.

Guardrails are actually "a system designed to keep vehicles from straying into dangerous or off-limit areas."

So they keep us *out* of danger . . . and *inside* the proper limits.

A Little Hurt Is Better than a Lot

The theory behind a guardrail is that you'll experience less injury to yourself, and maybe even less damage to your vehicle, if you strike a guardrail rather than crashing into something on the other side of it. The whole idea is that it's okay to cause a small amount of harm in order to keep from experiencing something worse.

And think about this. Many guardrails exclude us from areas where, theoretically at least, we *actually could drive.* But driving there could be bad news.

We don't pay much attention to guardrails until the moment comes when we need one. As we drive along, they're an invisible part of our traveling experience.

We're glad they're there—on bridges, in medians, and around curves—but for the most part, we pay no attention to them.

Bypassing Regrets

Guardrails. It's a concept that relates keenly to other areas of our lives.

Because chances are, if we'd had some form of guardrails established in a certain area, we could have avoided our greatest regrets in life. It might be something that hurt us financially, relationally, morally, or professionally. Whatever it was, and however much it hurt, it *might never have happened* if only we'd established some protective barriers.

The Tragic Results Nobody Wants

In our dangerous culture, we're all aware of certain destructive consequences, the kind we don't want in our lives.

If we could set up some guardrails that would always keep those tragic consequences on the other side of them—wouldn't that be worth it? Then whenever we bumped against them, they would keep us from destroying our lives.

We never *plan* to mess up, but it happens so easily when we fail to establish guardrails.

We shouldn't ignore this whole concept because we think, *Well, I just hope God will protect me.* Because God's protection for us actually comes through the guardrails he's given us throughout the Bible. Yes, he intends to protect us, and that's how.

To the Edge

What's sad is how we flirt with disaster in so many significant arenas of life. Many of us naturally assume we can play as close to the edge of the abyss as we want without experiencing harm. We like the thrill of just being there. And though we know about the danger (after all, that's why it's so thrilling), we don't *really* think we're personally at risk of falling.

We're so self-confident. But believe me, so were those who went over the cliff, right up until the moment they plunged uncontrollably into tragedy.

For the Future's Sake

Think about your future a moment. Can you imagine what it might be like if, from now on, you had adequate guardrails in place in all the significant areas of your life? We need them because our culture is baiting us to the edge of disaster, only to scold or punish us if we ever step across the line.

So let's stop flirting with disaster and take time now to set up the protections we need.

No one has ever regretted establishing a guardrail—but there are plenty of us who look back and regret not having them.

SESSION 1

Direct and Protect

Good fathers want to keep their children out of harm's way. So they set protective barriers, and they talk to their children about them. They establish rules and boundaries to keep their behavior from getting them too close to damaging consequences.

Isn't that exactly what a good father *should* do?

This fatherly approach is a big part of both the Old and New Testaments—just as we might expect, knowing how much God, our heavenly Father, loves us. He wants to keep his children away from life's danger zones. And in his goodness, he's done what it takes to help us do exactly that.

He knows the kinds of boundaries we need to set for ourselves. Are you willing to look at this with him, to hear the kind of help he wants to give you?

DISCUSSION STARTER

Have you ever been in a traffic accident (or seen one) where a vehicle hit a guardrail? If so, what function did the guardrail serve? What did it prevent?

How would you define a guardrail's purpose, in your own words?

VIDEO OVERVIEW

For Session 1 of the DVD

We can think of a guardrail as a *personal standard of behavior* that becomes a matter of conscience. Whenever we bump against these guardrails, we receive an internal warning.

In our culture there are behaviors that almost everyone agrees are bad—serious mistakes and dangerous actions to avoid—whether relationally, financially, morally, ethically, or professionally. Nevertheless, our culture's warning system can be very weak.

In fact, our culture doesn't like the kinds of guardrails we're talking about here. They're seen as stupid, silly rules—too confining and restrictive.

In the book of Ephesians, as he addressed people living in a culture even more immoral than ours, the apostle Paul lists several things people needed to be on their guard about. And to help them do this, he also uses the concept of guardrails.

He urged them to "be very careful" how they lived, reminding them that "the days are evil" (5:15–16). They were living in dangerous times, as we are today.

Paul adds, "Therefore do not be foolish, but understand what the Lord's will is" (5:17). He wants them to face up to God's will for their lives in every area.

The first illustration Paul gives of a guardrail concerns alcohol. He tells his readers not to get drunk, because it leads to debauchery—the kind of extreme indulgence that results in loss of control. Paul sets up the avoidance of drunkenness as a guardrail against something worse.

Throughout the Scriptures, we discover warnings to avoid whatever leads to this kind of loss of control in our lives—whether it's lust, drunkenness, greed, anger, gluttony, or whatever.

To emphasize his point, Paul presents a contrast. He says that instead of getting drunk, they should "be filled with the Spirit" (5:18).

Paul knows that our heavenly Father wants to be the preeminent influencer in our lives. And the Bible teaches that when we put our faith in Christ, the Spirit of God comes to live in us in a unique way, to prompt us, guide us, and direct us.

Paul is saying, *When you sense that still, small voice warning you on the inside, then pay attention. Be careful! Because your life's too important and time's too short and the world's too dangerous not to.*

VIDEO NOTES

_____

_____

_____

_____

_____

_____

_____

_____

_____

_____

_____

_____

_____

_____

_____

_____

_____

_____

_____

_____

DISCUSSION QUESTIONS

1. Andy defines a guardrail as "a personal standard of behavior that becomes a matter of conscience." Why is it important that we think of these guardrails *personally*—as something individually for us and not necessarily for everyone?

2. In establishing guardrails, why is it important that they be linked to our consciences?

3. What are the kinds of disasters and danger zones that you especially want to guard against—in your marriage and family, as well as financially, professionally, morally, ethically, relationally, and in other areas?

4. How can establishing guardrails help open us to the protective love of God?

5. What kind of protection from God should we be able to count on? What kind of protection from him should we not count on?

6. In various areas of your life, how strong is your desire to live by God's will and God's plan? How well do you know his will and his plan in each of these areas?

MILEPOSTS

- We all need to establish guardrails in significant areas of our lives. They protect us from the "danger zones," where the consequences are most destructive.

- Guardrails are valuable because they help us avoid the great regrets of life. All of us have areas of regret that could have been avoided if we'd established guardrails in those areas.

- A guardrail is a personal standard of behavior that becomes a matter of conscience. It's personal—meant just for us (and not as a rule that applies to everyone). And it involves the conscience, so that it triggers our sense of danger and brings a sense of guilt when we bump against it.

MOVING FORWARD

At this point, what is your attitude and response concerning the whole idea of establishing guardrails in your life? Is this something you see a need for? Why or why not?

CHANGING YOUR MIND

Allow this passage to help you focus on our highest aim when we establish guardrails:

Therefore do not be foolish,
but understand what the Lord's will is.
Ephesians 5:17

PREPARATION FOR SESSION 2

To help you prepare for Session 2, use these suggested devotions during the week leading up to your small group meeting.

Day One

Look at Proverbs 13:20. In your own words, how would you restate both the *promise* and the *warning* found in that verse?

Day Two

How does 1 Corinthians 15:33 relate to the truths you saw in Proverbs 13:20?

Day Three

Look at what we're told to do with others in Hebrews 10:24–25. To what extent does this happen when you are with your friends?

Day Four

Look also at what we're told to do with others in 1 Thessalonians 5:11. To what extent does this happen when you are with your friends?

Day Five

Look also at what we're told to do with others in Hebrews 3:13. To what extent does this happen when you are with your friends?

Last Session

A guardrail is a personal standard of behavior that becomes a matter of conscience. We need guardrails in every significant area of our lives, because they protect us from the "danger zones," where we're likely to be deeply hurt. These guardrails help us avoid the big regrets of life.

SESSION 2

Why Can't We Be Friends?

What makes friendship so great is the same thing that makes it so dangerous. With friends, we drop our guards. We're most open to influence from others when we're with people who accept us the way real friends do.

Acceptance leads to influence. And it can work for us—or against us. Some of the most addictive behaviors imaginable are those that people began as pastimes with friends.

Our friends greatly influence the direction and the quality of our lives. In fact, they can actually *determine* the direction and the quality of our lives. Think about it: how much have your friends impacted who you are?

Friendships are valuable. But because friendships can also be dangerous, we need guardrails.

DISCUSSION STARTER

Who are some of the most influential friends you've known, and how did they influence you? What did you appreciate most about them and their friendship? What did the relationships teach you about friendship?

In general, how would you describe the value of friendship?

VIDEO OVERVIEW

For Session 2 of the DVD

In the Bible, we see an important principle about friendship stated in an unmistakable way by Solomon. It's in Proverbs 13:20, which offers both a promise and a warning: "Walk with the wise and become wise, for a companion of fools suffers harm."

Solomon says that wisdom is contagious. If we surround ourselves with wise people, we too will become wise.

According to Scripture, a wise person is someone who understands that all of life is connected. He or she knows that what we do today—our decisions, thoughts, and actions—will influence who we are tomorrow. There are no isolated events or thought patterns or relationships or habits. They are all connected.

So, the wise person makes decisions based not simply on today, but on tomorrow and the day after.

The warning in Proverbs 13:20 is not that a companion of fools will become a fool himself. Rather, the companion of fools will eventually be hurt in some way by the fool's behavior. We might spend our entire lives with fools and never see the world in the same way they do or behave as they do. But eventually the shrapnel from the devastation in their lives will impact us, no matter how strong and disciplined we think we are.

Some of us have defended unhealthy relationships by thinking, *I'll never go along with the wrong things they participate in or the wrong things they believe; therefore, I'm safe.* Solomon would answer that by saying, *You're dead wrong, because the companion of fools will eventually be harmed by the outcome of the fool's behavior.*

The Bible describes a fool as someone who knows the difference between right and wrong but doesn't care. Fools live as if today has no bearing on tomorrow. If we have friends who don't care about their own lives, they won't be concerned about ours either.

If we ignore this principle, we will ultimately suffer the consequences. But if we leverage it to our benefit, we'll be rewarded.

In light of this principle, here are four suggested guardrails for friendships. These are things that should cause us concern, things that should bother us when we recognize them:

- When our core group of friends isn't moving in the direction we want our lives to go

- When we catch ourselves pretending to be someone other than who we know we are

- When we hear ourselves saying, *I'll go, but I won't participate*

- When we hope the people we care about most won't discover where we've been or who we've been with

These things should concern us to the point that we do something about them, rather than wait until there's a serious problem.

VIDEO NOTES

_____

_____

_____

_____

_____

_____

_____

_____

_____

_____

_____

_____

_____

_____

_____

_____

_____

_____

_____

_____

_____

_____

DISCUSSION QUESTIONS

1. How fully do you agree with this statement: "Our friends
    ultimately influence the direction and quality of our lives"?

2. As you see it, how strong is the connection between being
    accepted by others and being open to their influence?

3. If it's true that "friendships can be dangerous," how would
    you describe the danger?

4. How would you define "wisdom"? And what are the most important ways it can be learned from our friends?

5. If a fool can be biblically defined as "someone who knows the difference between right and wrong, but doesn't care," how can we discover whether this is actually true of someone we know?

6. What kind of pressure do you experience in your circle of friends? Is it mostly positive or negative?

MILEPOSTS

- We need guardrails in our friendships because our friends greatly impact the direction and quality of our lives. In many ways, they actually *determine* the direction and quality of our lives.

- Friendships are valuable. If we surround ourselves with friends who understand life's connectedness, we'll grow in our own understanding of this important truth.

- Friendships can also be dangerous. If we surround ourselves with friends who are fools—who *do not* understand life's connectedness—we'll be negatively impacted by the destructive consequences in their lives.

MOVING FORWARD

Take time to evaluate your circle of friends. Are they moving in the direction you want your life to go? When you're around them, do you find yourself pretending to be someone you really aren't? Do you feel pressure to compromise?

CHANGING YOUR MIND

Reflect on this session's key Scripture passage, and use it to deepen

your understanding of the dynamics of friendship.

Walk with the wise and become wise,
for a companion of fools suffers harm.
Proverbs 13:20

PREPARATION FOR SESSION 3

To help you prepare for Session 3, use these suggested devotions during the week leading up to your small group meeting.

Day One

Read 1 Corinthians 6:18–20. What are we commanded to do in the opening words of this passage? And what do you see as the significance of that command?

Day Two

Read 1 Corinthians 6:18–20. After the brief opening command in verse 18, one reason for that command is given in the rest of verse 18. How would you explain that reason in your own words?

Day Three

Read 1 Corinthians 6:18–20. What reason for fleeing sexual immorality is given in the first part of verse 19? How would you explain this in your own words?

Day Four

Read 1 Corinthians 6:18–20. What additional reasons for fleeing sexual immorality are given in the last part of verse 19 and in the first part of verse 20? How would you restate these in your own words?

Day Five

Read 1 Corinthians 6:18–20. Notice the command that is given in the last line in verse 20. What does this mean?

Last Session

Friendships are valuable, but they can also be dangerous. The right friends wisely understand life's connectedness, and they enable us to do the same. The wrong friends are fools who don't understand life's connectedness, and when their lives are shattered, the impact brings harm to us as well.

SESSION 3

Flee Baby Flee!

When it comes to establishing guardrails, there's one area more than any other where they are needed. Yet, it's the area where we find the most resistance to them. For some reason, we have a hard time facing up to this issue until we finally begin seeing it realistically.

Guardrails are needed in every area of our lives where we experience desire, but when it comes to sexual intimacy, we need the strongest and toughest guardrails.

In other areas of life—financially, educationally, professionally—we can fully recover from just about any kind of disaster, given enough time. We can eventually recover from our mistakes and failures; we learn from them and eventually even laugh about them.

But sexual disaster is almost impossible to fully recover from.

That's because we know intuitively that sex isn't just physical; it's much deeper than that. When people cross certain lines in their desire for physical intimacy, there are things they'll carry with them—the damage, the guilt, the ghosts—for the rest of their lives.

It goes on and on and on.

This is where all of us emphatically need guardrails.

DISCUSSION STARTER

How would you evaluate our culture's general approach to sexual intimacy? How do you see it influencing the people you know best? How has it influenced you?

VIDEO OVERVIEW

For Session 3 of the DVD

We would all be better off if we took this simple verse more seriously: "Flee from sexual immorality" (1 Corinthians 6:18). *Flee*—not "be careful" or "watch out." *Flee*. When it comes to sexual immorality, what could be any clearer?

Flee. This is exactly what we want our friends and family to do when it comes to sexual immorality. But when it comes to us, we often flirt rather than flee, don't we?

In all the areas where we need guardrails, our culture baits us to the edge of disaster, and then mocks us when we step over. This is especially true in the area of sexual immorality. Our culture isn't going to improve in this regard, so we need guardrails.

The Bible gives us great incentives for creating guardrails in this area. Paul asks, "Do you not know that your bodies are temples of the Holy Spirit, who is in you, whom you have received from God?" (1 Corinthians 6:19). He goes on: "You are not your own. You were bought at a price" (6:19–20). When Christ died for our sins, he purchased us from sin. We're no longer slaves to sin and to our desires and appetites. So Paul concludes with this application: "Therefore honor God with your bodies" (6:20).

Here are some specific guardrails to consider as we honor God with our bodies.

First, a list for married people:

1. Don't travel alone with someone of the opposite sex.

2. Don't eat alone or have coffee alone with someone of the opposite sex.

3. Don't hire "cute" members of the opposite sex because you want to help them.

4. Don't confide in or counsel someone of the opposite sex.

5. When you feel an attraction toward a specific person, tell someone immediately (not necessarily your spouse).

6. Make sure your spouse knows where your guardrails are so he or she can be comfortable with them and hold you accountable to them.

And for singles:

1. In any relationship with a married person of the opposite sex, don't travel alone or have meals alone with that person, and don't confide in or counsel that person.

2. No sleepovers.

3. In your social environment, if a date has become equivalent to having sex, then decide on a one-year break from relationships with the opposite sex. Use that time to allow God to renew your mind and heart.

VIDEO NOTES

_____

_____

_____

_____

_____

_____

_____

_____

_____

_____

_____

_____

_____

_____

_____

_____

_____

_____

_____

_____

_____

DISCUSSION QUESTIONS

1. In your own understanding, why do we especially need guardrails to protect us from sexual immorality? Why is this a strategic area for strengthening our own protections?

2. Without reavealing names, what examples can you give of people whose lives have been permanently altered by sexual immorality?

3. Why do you think our culture—and all of us, in general—is often so resistant to the idea of establishing protective barriers in this area?

4. Why exactly can we *not* expect our culture to become a healthier environment for promoting higher standards of sexual morality?

5. With a biblical perspective in mind, why is it so important to "flee from sexual immorality" (1 Corinthians 6:18)? Why is this kind of avoidance and escape so strategic and valuable?

6. What exactly does it mean to you to "honor God" with your body (as we're told to do in 1 Corinthians 6:20)?

MILEPOSTS

- We need stronger guardrails in the area of sexual intimacy than anywhere else in life, because sexual disaster has permanent consequences.

- The Bible is clear about sexual immorality: *Flee!* (1 Corinthians 6:18). We're to actively shun temptations to sexual immorality.

- There are a number of proven guardrails we can establish to help us in this area to honor God with our bodies.

MOVING FORWARD

Think carefully through the specific guardrails suggested by Andy in this session. Which ones do you need to immediately establish in your life? If you find yourself resisting some of them—why exactly is that? What other similar guidelines come to mind as being appropriate for you?

CHANGING YOUR MIND

Allow this biblical instruction to be a powerful motivation for you to

"flee from sexual immorality" (1 Corinthians 6:18).

Do you not know that your bodies are temples of the Holy Spirit,
who is in you, whom you have received from God?
You are not your own; you were bought at a price.
Therefore honor God with your bodies.
1 Corinthians 6:19–20

PREPARATION FOR SESSION 4

To help you prepare for Session 4, use these suggested devotions during the week leading up to your small group meeting.

Day One

Proverbs 27:12 is a "guardrail" verse. Look it up, and think about its meaning. How could you apply it in prayer, asking for God's help? And how could it apply in helping you establish guardrails in your life?

Day Two

A potential "guardrail" verse is Proverbs 4:23. For this verse, answer the same questions as you did in Day One for Proverbs 27:12.

Day Three

Another guardrail passage to consider is Psalm 119:9–11. For this passage, answer the questions for Day One.

Day Four

A passage to conisder is 1 Corinthians 6:12. Again, apply to this verse the questions for Day One.

Day Five

Another passage to consider is 1 Corinthians 10:31. Again, apply to this verse the questions given in Day One.

Last Session

Flee sexual immorality—that's a clear biblical principle that should govern our behavior in responding to sexual temptation.

SESSION 4

Me and the Mrs.

Maybe setting up guardrails in your life sounds like a wise thing to do, but you're thinking it's easier said than done. Especially if you're a husband or a wife, and you're thinking through how the two of you can approach this whole concept together.

DISCUSSION STARTER

Among the couples you know, what good examples have you seen of deciding on protective strategies together to ensure the health and vitality of their marriages?

VIDEO OVERVIEW

For Session 4 of the DVD

Guardrails not only protect; they also direct. They guide us in discerning the will of God.

Establishing and living by guardrails earns respect from others who appreciate personal standards.

Proverbs 27:12 is a guardrail verse: "The prudent see danger and take refuge, but the simple keep going and suffer for it." From it comes this prayer:

"Lord, help us see danger coming before it gets here; and as we see it, give us the wisdom to know what to do and the courage to do it."

Inappropriate relationships at work can have undesirable effects on our homes and families. So, another guardrail is for managers and executives to solicit their spouses' feedback and buy-in on their hiring decisions. There's normally a high wall dividing work and home, but what happens emotionally and relationally at work crosses over in its impact on the home. So why not bring down that wall by inviting that kind of involvement from spouses?

"Small groups" at church offer another relational guardrail. The relationships built there—through sharing life together, praying together, and exploring God's Word together—will quickly offer deep support, accountability, and friendship.

Wise financial guardrails in marriage include recording all expenses, deciding up-front what percentage of our income to live on (allowing for margin, avoiding debt, and being generous), and deciding to make *giving* a priority. Giving first is a guardrail against the assumption that all our income is for our own consumption—thus breaking the power of greed.

In the ongoing tension between work and home, another guardrail is choosing to let it be our professions that suffer, not our families—since there isn't really enough time to fully satisfy both. An example would be choosing to return home each day at a set time agreed to by both husband and wife.

Another guardrail is to diligently guard our schedules in order to focus on the primary task God has called us to—the kind of focus Nehemiah displayed when others tried to sidetrack him and he responded, "I am doing a great work and I cannot come down" (Nehemiah 6:3 NASB).

Another is for a couple to maintain a marriage-centered family, not a kids-centered family, with adequate time for just the two of them to continue nurturing their relationship.

VIDEO NOTES

_____

_____

_____

_____

_____

_____

_____

_____

_____

_____

_____

_____

_____

_____

_____

_____

_____

_____

_____

_____

_____

DISCUSSION QUESTIONS

1. "Guardrails not only protect; they also direct." Explain how you see that working. How can guardrails function practically to help us discover God's guidance?

2. Do you respect people who establish and live by the kinds of guardrails we've discussed in this series? Why or why not?

3. What are some ways we can more clearly recognize approaching danger as it confronts our marriages or families or other relationships? Or as it threatens our personal or professional lives?

4. What accountability, support, encouragement, and friend-ship can you count on from those outside your family?

5. What do you see as the most important factors for couples to consider as they guard their finances?

6. What do you see as the most important factors for couples to consider as they guard the use of their time?

MILEPOSTS

- Guardrails have proven value. Guardrails not only protect; they also *direct*. By establishing strong guardrails, we allow ourselves to more easily receive guidance and direction from God.

- As a key guardrail verse, Proverbs 27:12 helps us understand the need to protect ourselves from approaching danger, rather than casually continuing forward and encountering negative consequences.

- The right guardrails help us make the best use of our finances and our time, as well as strengthening our families and other relationships.

MOVING FORWARD

What do you find most encouraging from the things that Sandra and Andy have learned and applied in their marriage and family? If you're married, in what ways do you identify with them? In what way is your marriage different (not better or worse; just different) from theirs? What can you learn from them? What do you think they might be able to learn from you?

CHANGING YOUR MIND

Adopt this verse into protective thinking and strategies for yourself

and your family:

The prudent see danger and take refuge,
but the simple keep going and pay the penalty.
Proverbs 27:12

PREPARATION FOR SESSION 5

To help you prepare for Session 5, use these suggested devotions during the week leading up to your small group meeting.

Day One

Read the words of Jesus in Matthew 6:24. What truths does this passage uncover about our loyalty, devotion, and service?

Day Two

Continue reading Jesus' words in Matthew 6:25–30. What important truth is Jesus trying to teach us about God?

Day Three

Continue in this passage, this time reading Matthew 6:31–32, where Jesus sums up what he has been saying in the previous verses. How would you summarize it in your own words?

Day Four

Read Matthew 6:33. What is Jesus asking us to do here? And what promise does he make?

Day Five

Finally, read Matthew 6:34. What further emphasis does this passage give to the whole point of what you've been reading in Matthew
6:24–33?

Last Session

Guardrails have proven their protective value repeatedly. And they help *direct* us as well as protect us—they open us up to a clearer discernment of God's will. In our finances, our use of time, our family relationships, and many other areas, guardrails bring an order and security to life that we otherwise would miss.

SESSION 5

The Consumption Assumption

Most of our worst crises in life and most of our greatest regrets have to do with either sex or money. Yet, our culture usually dismisses anything Scripture has to say about these topics.

We looked earlier at one of those tough issues; now let's tackle the other. What do you need to be on your guard about when it comes to finances?

The Bible has a great deal to say on this topic. And it all comes back to one simple thing.

The reason God says so much about it actually has nothing to do with money; it has everything to do with *devotion*. God knows that his chief competition for our hearts and our devotion—for our loyalty, our fellowship, and our service—is not the devil, but rather our wealth and consumption.

God knows that if he can control your money, he has your heart—because (as Jesus taught), where your treasure is, that's where your heart is also.

When it comes to your finances, what needs guarding is not your cash, but your heart.

DISCUSSION STARTER

In your approach to finances, do you think of yourself as more of a saver or a spender? If you're married, how would you categorize your spouse?

VIDEO OVERVIEW

For Session 5 of the DVD

Jesus says, "No one can serve two masters. Either you will hate the one and love the other, or you will be devoted to the one and despise the other. *You cannot serve both God and Money*" (Matthew 6:24).

We're in tension about whether to place our trust in God or in money and the pursuit of wealth (and whatever money can buy).

As we think about our need for guardrails in this area, there are ditches on both sides of our paths when it comes to finances: consumption and hoarding. Most of us don't want to be hoarders; we're fine with being consumers. But consuming, strictly speaking, means the consumption of everything that comes our way. Meanwhile, hoarding happens because we're anxiously asking, *What if I get sick and can't work? What if the economy gets worse? What if, what if, what if?*

Both the consumer and the hoarder are self-centered; both live as if there is no God; and both are fueled by greed. Greed is simply the assumption that anything coming to us is for our own consumption—either now or later.

We can believe in God yet still be fueled by greed if finances are our chief concern and the object of our ultimate dependence. And when we face financial difficulties, we're quick to ask God for help. God is like our backup financial plan. He's on the periphery.

But the Bible tells us that God wants to be the master and ruler of our lives, not our backup plan.

The key to breaking the power of greed is simple. It's a habit we develop through our decision to allow our heavenly Father to rule our lives. That habit is described in just three words: give, save, live.

That's the order of priority. When we are paid, the first thing we do is give a percentage away. This is saying, *God, I will not be ruled by my stuff. I will not be owned by the things I own. My hands are open. The first percentage goes to you.*

Jesus later tells us not to worry about the things we truly need that money can buy. When we worry like that, we're living as if God isn't aware and doesn't care.

One of the biggest decisions we can make is to affirm for all time that God knows and God cares. Then we will begin changing our orientations from stuff-centered to God-centered, as we continually seek his help in managing our lives and finances.

Then we're free to carry out the pursuit Jesus calls us to: "Seek first his kingdom [that is, God's purpose and will] and his righteousness [God's values, God's understanding of right and wrong], and all these things [those needs that we worry about] will be given to you as well" (Matthew 6:33).

VIDEO NOTES

_____

_____

_____

_____

_____

_____

_____

_____

_____

_____

_____

_____

_____

_____

_____

_____

_____

_____

_____

_____

_____

_____

DISCUSSION QUESTIONS

1. In your own life, in what ways do you see money and the pursuit of wealth (or whatever wealth promises to buy, such as security or pleasure) as competitors to your devotion to God?

2. Do you sense a tension between your approach to finances and your love of God? If so, how would you describe it?

3. In practical terms, what's your understanding of greed? What's at the root of it?

4. In what ways (if any) are finances a major, ongoing concern in your life?

5. How would you say your approach to finances affects your desire to know God's purpose and will?

6. How would you say your approach to finances affects your openness to understanding God's values and standards?

MILEPOSTS

- Our urgent need for guardrails in the area of our finances is reflected in the fact that God has so much to say in the Bible about the role of money in our lives.

- Money is the leading competitor in our hearts to our devotion to God. Jesus makes it clear that none of us can be devoted to both God and money. Our tendency to be greedy is deep-rooted.

- To counter our tendency toward greed, the most practical guardrail in the area of our finances is to develop the habit of *give, save, live* as our system of financial priorities.

MOVING FORWARD

How conscious are you of the fact that God fully *knows* all your needs (including your financial needs), and that he completely *cares* for you and is entirely committed to meeting all your true needs? Is this something you have already affirmed to him in prayer? Is that something you need to do now?

CHANGING YOUR MIND

The words of Jesus in this passage are well known for their liberating power and perspective. Take them to heart as they relate to your own financial needs.

But seek first his kingdom and his righteousness,
and all these things will be given to you as well.
Matthew 6:33

PREPARATION FOR SESSION 6

To help you prepare for Session 6, use these suggested devotions during the week leading up to your small group meeting.

Day One

Open your Bible to the book of Daniel. What important background information to Daniel's story is given in the first seven verses of chapter 1?

Day Two

What important decision does Daniel make in verse 8 of chapter 1? How would you explain the significance of this?

Day Three

Read Daniel 1:9–14. What "test" does Daniel propose, and how is it put into place? How do these verses demonstrate Daniel's trust in God?

Day Four

What was the outcome of the test that Daniel proposed, according to verses 15–16 in chapter 1?

Day Five

What were the further consequences of Daniel's action, according to Daniel 1:17–21?

Last Session

God's leading competitor to our heart's devotion is our devotion to money, which is deeply rooted in our tendency toward greed. But we can counter that tendency by establishing a practical guardrail—by practicing the habit of *give, save, live* as our system of financial priorities.

SESSION 6

Once and for All

Here's our big pushback to establishing guardrails: "They'll keep me from something I want. They'll be in my way."

But guardrails or no guardrails, the tension we feel isn't going away. The temptations will be there. Eliminating guardrails will only erode our resolve and bring us to a place of temptation where the consequences are much worse. Not having guardrails just moves the battle line closer to disaster.

Our desires and appetites are never fully and finally satisfied. They always come back for more. We shouldn't deceive ourselves into thinking that by saying yes, yes, yes, yes, yes, we'll never have to say no.

There's someone in Scripture who knew all this and demonstrated what it can mean in one of the most dramatic life stories in all of history.

DISCUSSION STARTER

If you're familiar with the story of Daniel in the Bible, what do you re-call most from his life? What impresses you most about him?

VIDEO OVERVIEW

For Session 6 of the DVD

In 605 BC, Daniel and his three friends Hananiah, Mishael, and Aza-riah (also known as Shadrach, Meshach, and Abednego) were among the Jewish nobles taken captive to Babylon by King Nebuchadnez-zar. There they were to undergo a three-year process of being indoc-trinated and reoriented to Babylonian culture before they entered the king's service. As Daniel realized, this would mean being slowly stripped of their beliefs and values.

So, Daniel "resolved not to defile himself with the royal food and wine, and he asked the chief official [whose name was Asphenaz] for permission not to defile himself this way" (Daniel 1:8).

Then we read, "*Now God* had caused the official to show favor and compassion to Daniel" (Daniel 1:9). Daniel knew that God uses our guardrails not only to protect us, but also to direct us.

Because of Daniel's resolve, what happens from this point on in his story is amazing. Daniel's decision to draw a line in the sand was the thing God used to direct his entire life. If he hadn't made this decision, we wouldn't have a book in the Bible called Daniel.

More than he could possibly imagine, everything hinged on his decision whether to eat the royal meat and drink the royal wine. Daniel said no—and God essentially responded, "This is your defining moment. I'm going to direct your entire future by this decision."

That experience is similar for many people. God becomes most real to them—and they discover the clearest direction in their lives— not when they're praying for his direction, but in moments of temptation and trials, moments of tension when they decide, *This is where I draw the line; this is as far as I'll go.* They later look back and realize, *That's the decision God used to completely redirect my life.* They were just trying to make the right ethical or moral decision, and God used it not only to protect them, but also to direct them.

Daniel had no idea what hung in the balance with his decision. We also have no idea what hangs in the balance of our decisions to establish guardrails for our lives. But later we'll be able to look back and say, "That was a defining moment. God redirected my entire life because I made up my mind."

In Daniel's story, God honored his decision. It was the beginning of a journey for his friends and him that would profoundly impact the nation of Israel. And it all started with a simple decision to say, "That's as far as I'll go."

VIDEO NOTES

_____

_____

_____

_____

_____

_____

_____

_____

_____

_____

_____

_____

_____

_____

_____

_____

_____

_____

_____

_____

DISCUSSION QUESTIONS

1. Are you experiencing any kind of continuing resistance to the idea of guardrails in your life? If so, how would you describe this resistance? And how would you explain the reason for it?

2. We all know the pressure and tension we feel when we encounter temptation. Can yielding to the temptation eliminate that feeling? Explain your understanding of this.

3. How have you personally seen the truth of this statement: "Our appetites are never fully and finally satisfied; they always come back wanting more"?

4. Do you think of establishing guardrails as a "defining mo-
    ment" in your life? If so, in what way?

5. What further help do you want or feel you need in establish-
    ing strong guardrails?

6. What have you learned most in this series about the impor-
    tance and value of guardrails?

MILEPOSTS

- We might resist the idea of guardrails, but there's no escaping the tension we'll continue to feel as we encounter temptations in every area of life. Yielding to temptation only increases the effects of the consequences later on.

- The levels of temptations will increase because in this life we never reach a point of having our desires and appetites fully satisfied.

- The story of Daniel dramatically illustrates the amazing destiny that unfolds for those who learn to draw the line, who in the face of temptation learn to say: *I refuse to go further.*

MOVING FORWARD

Have you made up your mind to keep and maintain guardrails in all the significant areas of your life? Have you resolved to draw the line in these areas and say, "That's as far as I'll go"? If so, what is your motivation for doing so, in light of your heavenly Father's loving care and control over your life?

CHANGING YOUR MIND

Reflect on these words, and ask God to allow you to experience the kind of integrity, uprightness, and guidance that the first line speaks of:

The integrity of the upright guides them,
but the unfaithful are destroyed by their duplicity.
Proverbs 11:3

Leader's Guide

So, You're the Leader...

Is that intimidating? Perhaps exciting? No doubt you have some mental pictures of what it will look like, what you will say, and how it will go. Before you get too far into the planning process, there are some things you should know about leading a small group discussion. We've compiled some tried and true techniques here to help you.

Basics About Leading

1. Cultivate discussion — It's easy to think that the meeting lives or dies by your ideas. In reality, the ideas of everyone in the group are what make a small group meeting successful. The most valuable thing you can do is to get people to share their thoughts. That's how the relationships in your group will grow and thrive. Here's a rule: The impact of your study material will typically never exceed the impact of the relationships through which it was studied. The more meaningful the relationships, the more meaningful the study. In a sterile environment, even the best material is suppressed.

2. Point to the material — A good host or hostess gets the party going by offering delectable hors d'oeuvres and beverages. You too should be ready to serve up "delicacies" from the material. Sometimes you will simply read the discussion questions and invite everyone to respond. At other times, you will encourage others to share their ideas. Remember, some of the best treats are the ones your guests will bring to the party. Go with the flow of the meeting, and be ready to pop out of the kitchen as needed.

3. Depart from the material — A talented ministry team has carefully designed this study for your small group. But that doesn't mean you should follow every part word for word. Knowing how and when to depart from the material is a valuable art. Nobody knows more about your people than you do. The narratives, questions, and exercises are here to provide a framework for discovery. However, every group is motivated differently. Sometimes the best way to start a small group discussion is simply to ask, "Does anyone have a personal insight or revelation they'd like to share from this week's material?" Then sit back and listen.

4. Stay on track — Conversation is the currency of a small group discussion. The more interchange, the healthier the "economy." However, you need to keep your objectives in mind. If your goal is to have a meaningful experience with this material, then you should make sure the discussion is contributing to that end. It's easy to get off on a tangent. Be prepared to interject politely and refocus the group. You might need to say something like, "Excuse me, we're obviously all interested in this subject; however, I just want to make sure we cover all the material for this week."

5. Above all, pray — The best communicators are the ones that manage to get out of God's way enough to let him communicate *through* them. That's important to keep in mind. Books don't teach God's Word; neither do sermons nor group discussions. God himself speaks into the hearts of men and women, and prayer is our vital channel to communicate directly with him. Cover your efforts in prayer. You don't just want God present at your meeting; you want him to direct it.

We hope you find these suggestions helpful. And we hope you enjoy leading this study. You will find additional guidelines and suggestions for each session in the Leader's Guide notes that follow.

Leader's Guide
Session Notes

Session 1 — Direct and Protect

Bottom Line

To help us avoid major regrets in the future, we need to set up protective guardrails in every significant area of our lives. These guardrails are personal standards of behavior that become a matter of conscience. They'll protect us from the "danger zones" of behavior that can so easily lead to disastrous consequences.

Discussion Starter

Use the "Discussion Starter" printed in Session 1 of the Participant's Guide to "break the ice"—and to help everyone recognize the obvious benefits of guardrails.

Notes for Discussion Questions

1. **Andy defines a guardrail as "a personal standard of behavior that becomes a matter of conscience." Why is it important that we think of these guardrails *personally*—as something individually for us and not necessarily for everyone?**

Guide the discussion toward greater recognition and understanding that these standards represent our personal understanding and convictions, *not* universal rules.

2.   **In establishing guardrails, why is it important that they be
      linked to our consciences?**

      In this discussion, help foster awareness that our consciences
      can be informed and energized by these guardrails.

3.   **What kinds of disasters and danger zones do you especially
      want to guard against—in your marriage and family, as well
      as financially, professionally, morally, ethically, relationally,
      and in other areas?**

      We probably prefer not to think how disastrous the conse-
      quences can be for wrong behavior, so use this question to
      help everyone face those facts honestly.

4.   **How can establishing guardrails help open us to the protec-
      tive love of God?**

      Guardrails that are rooted in our convictions based on biblical
      principles are indeed a blessing made possible only by God's
      grace. Help guide the discussion toward recognizing this truth.

5. **What kind of protection from God should we be able to count on? What kind of protection from him should we not count on?**

   Use the discussion to help counter the thought that we don't need guardrails if we simply decide: *I'll rely on God to protect me.*

6. **In various areas of your life, how strong is your desire to live by God's will and God's plan? How well do you know his will and his plan in each of these areas?**

   You might want to use this question as a springboard into deeper discussion of Ephesians 5:15–18.

Moving Forward

The goal here is to help the group become familiar with the concept and value of guardrails as they apply to the way we live our lives.

Preparation for Session 2

Remember to point out the brief daily devotions that the group members can complete and which will help greatly in stimulating discussion in your next session. These devotions will enable everyone to dig into the Bible and start wrestling with the topics that will come up next time.

Session 2 — Why Can't We Be Friends?

Bottom Line

Despite the great value of friendships, they can be dangerous, because our friends have so much influence over us—for bad as well as for good. That's why we need guardrails in our friendships to help us recognize when their influence is not as healthy as it should be.

Discussion Starter

Use the "Discussion Starter" listed for Session 2 of the Participant's Guide. This one should help everyone in your group focus on the value of friendship. It's definitely something that's worth protecting, and experiencing in the right way!

Notes for Discussion Questions

1. **How fully do you agree with this statement: "Our friends ultimately influence the direction and the quality of our lives"?** Some who view themselves as more independently minded might not agree with this statement. And, indeed, some of us are more impressionable than others. But the influence of friends is still far more powerful than we often realize.

2. **As you see it, how strong is the connection between being *accepted* by others and being open to their influence?**

    The discussion here can help everyone realize that the group of friends we've grown comfortable with might not be the best people for us to be around. There are many more things to seek in friendships than just our own comfort and sense of acceptance.

3. **If it's true that "friendships can be dangerous," how would you describe the danger?**

    Some in the group might be able to testify to the destructive influence of some of their friends in the past.

4. **How would you define "wisdom"? And what are the most important ways that it can be learned from our friends?**

    You might want to bring in the definition mentioned in the teaching session—that a wise person is one who sees the connectedness of life (our todays have been shaped by our choices yesterday, and our tomorrows will be determined by our choices today)—and who makes decisions based on that truth.

5.   **If a fool can be biblically defined as "someone who knows the difference between right and wrong, but doesn't care," how can we discover whether this is actually true of someone we know?**

   This should prompt some interesting discussion as everyone thinks about friends whose actions have proven to be unwise.

6.   **What kind of pressure do you experience in your circle of friends? Is it mostly positive or negative?**

   Some in your group might be surprised once they honestly recognize and evaluate this pressure.

Moving Forward

All of us have a sense of loyalty to our friends, even when they disappoint us. The goal here is to help the group see beyond that and to move toward an honest evaluation of how healthy our friendships really are.

Preparation for Session 3

Again, encourage your group members to complete the brief daily devotions. These will help stimulate discussion in your next session. They'll enable everyone to dig into the Bible and start wrestling with the topics coming up next time.

Session 3 — Flee Baby Flee!

Bottom Line

We need stronger guardrails in the area of sexual temptation than anywhere else in life. And all our guardrails in this area should reflect the Bible's core teaching: "Flee from sexual immorality" (1 Corinthians 6:18). We need all the help we can get to escape sexual temptation.

Discussion Starter

Again, use the "Discussion Starter" listed for Session 3 of the Participant's Guide. This should help the group focus on the dangers and deceptions in our culture's approach to sexuality.

Notes for Discussion Questions

1. **In your own understanding, why do we especially need guardrails to protect us from sexual immorality? Why is this a strategic area for strengthening our own protections?**

    A number of factors mentioned in the teaching session touch on the uniqueness of this area. You might want to review these things with the group.

2. **Without revealing names, what examples can you give of people whose lives have been permanently altered by sexual immorality?**

   The goal here is to help everyone honestly recognize the severe and lasting impact of sexual immorality.

3. **Why do you think our culture—and all of us, in general—is often so resistant to the idea of establishing protective barriers in this area?**

   Encourage a wide-open discussion and evaluation about this. There might be a number of ideas mentioned.

4. **Why exactly can we not expect our culture to become a healthier environment for promoting higher standards of sexual morality?**

   Help them recognize and face up to our culture's corruption.

5. **With a biblical perspective in mind, why is it so important to "flee from sexual immorality" (1 Corinthians 6:18)? Why is this kind of avoidance and escape so strategic and valuable?**

   Encourage the group toward a stronger trust in God's wisdom

in this area. He knows what's best for us to do in response to sexual temptation.

6. **What exactly does it mean to you to "honor God" with your body (as we're told to do in 1 Corinthians 6:20)?**

This might lead naturally to a deeper discussion of 1 Corinthians 6:18–20.

Moving Forward

The goal here is to make positive, deliberate progress toward establishing strong guardrails in this crucial area.

Preparation for Session 4

Again, encourage your group members to complete the daily devotions. This will help them be better prepared for the topics coming up next time.

Session 4 — Me and The Mrs.

Bottom Line

Guardrails have proven value, as Andy and Sandra Stanley can positively testify. Their encouraging example in the use of guardrails offers us insight in several dimensions.

Discussion Starter

Use the "Discussion Starter" listed for Session 4 of the Participant's Guide. This should help everyone focus on looking to couples with healthy marriages for good examples of guardrails

Notes for Discussion Questions

1. **"Guardrails not only protect; they also direct." Explain how you see that working. How can guardrails function practically to help us discover God's guidance?**

   Encourage a wider appreciation of the many benefits of guardrails.

2. **Do you respect people who establish and live by the kinds of guardrails we've discussed in this series? Why or why not?**

   While we're generally not attracted to people who seem legalistic, there's often a strong attraction to people with wise convictions and standards. Help everyone see the difference.

3. **What are some ways we can more clearly recognize approaching danger as it confronts our marriages or families or other relationships? Or as it threatens our personal or professional lives?**

    Bring in Proverbs 27:12 for discussion here.

4. **What accountability, support, encouragement, and friendship can you count on from those outside your family?**

    Hopefully, this group will be growing in providing these very things for one another.

5. **What do you see as the most important factors for couples to consider as they guard their finances?**

    The guidelines from Andy and Sandra should be especially helpful here.

6. **What do you see as the most important factors for couples to consider as they guard the use of their time?**

    Again, the guidelines mentioned in the teaching session by Andy and Sandra should lead to good discussion here.

Moving Forward

The goal here is simply to encourage lingering reflection and remembrance concerning the things shared by Andy and Sandra in the teaching session.

Preparation for Session 5

Again, encourage your group members to complete the daily devotions in preparation for the next session.

Session 5 — The Consumption Assumption

Bottom Line

There are no greater threats to our devotion to God—our loyalty, fellowship, and service toward him—than money and the pursuit of wealth. That's why we need strong guardrails in this area. One of the strongest is the simple priority pattern of *give, save, live* as a habit in determining how we allocate our money.

Discussion Starter

Use the "Discussion Starter" listed for Session 5 of the Participant's Guide. This should help the group focus on the different perspectives from which we view finances.

Notes for Discussion Questions

1. **In your own life, in what ways do you see money and the pursuit of wealth (or whatever wealth promises to buy, such as security or pleasure) as competitors to your devotion to God?**

    Many in your group might be resistant to recognizing this truth in their lives. It would be helpful to approach it from various angles.

2. **Do you sense a tension between your approach to finances and your love of God? If so, how would you describe it?**

   Many will experience this, and the tension manifests itself in various ways. Explore this thoroughly.

3. **In practical terms, what's your understanding of greed? What's at the root of it?**

   Refer back to the definition supplied in the teaching session: greed is simply our assumption that anything coming to us is for our own consumption—either now or later.

4. **In what ways (if any) are finances a major, ongoing concern in your life?**

   For some, finances will represent a constant source of anxiety. Yet there will likely be a reluctance to admit this. Answering this very candidly yourself will help others to do the same.

5. **How would you say your approach to finances affects your desire to know God's purpose and will?**

   This is a good time to bring in the command of Jesus in Matthew 6:33 about seeking first the kingdom of God.

6. **How would you say your approach to finances affects your openness to understand God's values and standards?**

The words of Jesus in Matthew 6:33 are relevant, especially concerning our need to seek God's righteousness.

Moving Forward

Encourage your group to positively affirm for themselves the stunning reality of God's goodness and greatness in how he actively cares for us in all our needs.

Preparation for Session 6

Encourage your group members to complete the daily devotions in preparation for the next session.

Session 6 — Once and for All

Bottom Line

Our need for guardrails is accentuated by the fact that our various desires and appetites will never reach a point of being fully satisfied. Daniel's example in the Bible shows us the urgent need to draw a line and say, "I refuse to go further" in certain areas of our lives. The result will be a destiny that opens us up to God's amazing guidance and provision.

Discussion Starter

Once more, use the "Discussion Starter" listed for Session 6 of the Participant's Guide. This should help everyone in the group to focus on the exemplary value of Daniel's story in the Bible as it relates to guardrails.

Notes for Discussion Questions

1. **Are you experiencing any kind of continuing resistance to the idea of guardrails in your life? If so, how would you describe this resistance? And how would you explain the reason for it?** Allow plenty of time to discuss this. Encourage honest answers, and demonstrate positive acceptance toward anyone who's struggling with applying guardrails.

2.   **We all know the pressure and tension we feel when we en-
     counter temptation. Can yielding to the temptation eliminate
     that feeling? Explain your understanding of this.**

     Refer back to the points made about this in the teaching ses-
     sions. The answer is definitely no, but it will help us greatly if we
     understand why.

3.   **How have you personally seen the truth of this statement:
     "Our appetites are never fully and finally satisfied; they al-
     ways come back wanting more"?**

     Most, if not all, of us have come to recognize this unattractive
     truth. It might seem discouraging—but the Bible is full of encour-
     agement and truth in our fight against temptation.

4.   **Do you think of establishing guardrails as a "defining mo-
     ment" in your life? If so, in what way?**

     Obviously, this will become fully clear only in the future; nev-
     ertheless, it's encouraging to have a strong vision of what can
     happen later if we faithfully set up guardrails now.

5. **What further help do you want or feel you need in establishing strong guardrails in your life?**

    Spend plenty of time here. Obviously, these teaching sessions do not deal with all the issues associated with our need for guardrails. There's much more we can learn and apply. Encourage one another in a lifelong pursuit of these discoveries.

6. **What have you learned most in this series about the importance and value of guardrails?**

    Again, allow plenty of time for all group members to review the series highlights and to articulate a big picture view of what this series has meant for them.

Moving Forward

The goal here is to encourage a strong sense of vision of the good things that can happen in the future when we're faithful now to establish strong guardrails.

Taking Responsibility for Your Life DVD

Because Nobody Else Will

Andy Stanley

RESPONSIBILITIES.

We all have them. But we don't all take them as seriously as we ought to. Wouldn't it be great, though, if we all took responsibility for the things we are responsible for? Wouldn't it be great if you took responsibility for everything you're responsible for? It's time to stop the finger-pointing and excuse-making and to remove the "ir" in irresponsible.

In this 4-part study, Andy Stanley tells us it's time to ask ourselves, "Am I REALLY taking responsibility for my life?"

Session titles:
1. Let the Blames Begin
2. The Disproportionate Life
3. This Is No Time to Pray
4. Embracing Your Response Ability

Designed for use with the *Taking Responsibility for Your Life Participant's Guide*.

Your Move

Four Questions to Ask When You Don't Know What to Do

Andy Stanley

We are all faced with decisions that we never anticipated having to make. And, we usually have to make them quickly. In this four session video group study, author and pastor Andy Stanley discusses four questions that will help participants make sound decisions with God's help. Follow Andy as he teaches how every decision and its outcomes become a permanent part of your story, what to do when you feel the need to pause before taking action, and how to make more of this life by making sound decisions.

The DVD-ROM and separate participant's guide contain everything you need to create your group experience:

Staying in Love

Falling in Love Is Easy, Staying in Love Requires a Plan

Andy Stanley

We all know what's required to fall in love…a pulse. Falling in love is easy. But staying there—that's something else entirely. With more than a thousand matchmaking services available today and new ones springing up all the time, finding a romantic match can be easier than ever. But staying together with the one you've found seems to be the real challenge.

So, is it possible for two people to fall in love and actually stay there? Absolutely! Let pastor and author Andy Stanley show you how in this four-session, video-based study that also features a separate participant's guide.

Session titles include:

1. The Juno Dilemma
2. Re-Modeling
3. Feelin' It
4. Multiple Choice Marriage

Faith, Hope, and Luck

Discover What You Can Expect from God

Andy Stanley

Our faith in God often hinges on his activity—or inactivity—in our daily experiences. When our prayers are answered, our faith soars. When God is silent, it becomes harder to trust him. When God shows up in an unmistakable way, our confidence in him reaches new heights. But when he doesn't come through, our confidence often wanes.

But it doesn't have to be that way—it's not supposed to be that way.

This five-session study is guaranteed to transform your thinking about faith. As you listen or watch, you will discover the difference between faith and hope. You will be presented with a definition of faith that will shed new light on both the Old and New Testaments. Andy Stanley explains what we can expect of God every time we come to him with a request. In addition, he exposes the flaws in what some have labeled The Faith Movement.

With both a DVD and separate participant's guide, *Faith, Hope, and Luck* is not just another group study. This content is foundational for everyone who desires to be an informed, active follower of Christ.

Five sessions include:

1. Better Odds
2. Betting on Hope
3. Beating the Odds
4. No Dice
5. All In

Five Things God Uses to Grow Your Faith

Andy Stanley

Imagine how different your outlook on life would be if you had absolute confidence that God was with you. Imagine how differently you would respond to difficulties, temptations, and even good things if you knew with certainty that God was in all of it and was planning to leverage it for good. In other words, imagine what it would be like to have PERFECT faith. In this DVD study, Andy Stanley builds a biblical case for five things God uses to grow BIG faith.

In six video sessions, Andy covers the following topics:

- Big Faith
- Practical Teaching
- Providential Relationships
- Private Disciplines
- Personal Ministry
- Pivotal Circumstances

Along with the separate participant's guide, this resource will equip groups to become more mature followers of Jesus Christ.

Available in stores and online!

Twisting the Truth

Learning to Discern in a Culture of Deception

Andy Stanley

   In six insight-packed sessions, Andy Stanley exposes four destructive and all-too-prevalent lies about authority, pain, sex, and sin. They're deceptions powerful enough to ruin our relationships, our lives, even our eternities—but only if we let them. Including both a small group DVD and participant's guide that work together, *Twisting the Truth* untwists the lies that can drag us down. With his gift for straight, to-the-heart communication, Andy Stanley helps us exchange falsehoods for truths that can turn our lives completely around.

Starting Point Starter Kit

Find Your Place in the Story

Andy Stanley and the Starting Point Team

Starting Point is an exploration of God's grand story and where you fit into the narrative. This proven, small group experience is carefully designed to meet the needs of

- Seekers that are curious about Christianity
- Starters that are new to a relationship with Jesus
- Returners that have been away from church for a while

Starting Point is an accepting, conversational environment where people learn about God's story and their places in it. Starting Point helps participants explore the Bible and begin to understand key truths of the Christian faith.

Carefully refined to enhance community, the ten interactive sessions in Starting Point encourage honest exploration. The *Conversation Guide*, which includes a five-disk audio series featuring Andy Stanley, helps each participant enjoy and engage fully with the small group experience.

About This Starter Kit

The *Starting Point Starter Kit* is geared for ministry leaders. It consists of the following:

- Four-color *Starting Point Conversation Guide* containing five audio disks, with over five hours of teaching by Andy Stanley
- *Starter Guide* providing step-by-step instructions on how to successfully launch and sustain the Starting Point ministry
- A Starting Point TNIV Bible
- One-hour leader training DVD
- Interactive CD containing promotional videos, pre-service marketing graphics, leader training tools, and administrative resources

Share Your Thoughts

With the Author: Your comments will be forwarded to the author when you send them to *zauthor@zondervan.com*.

With Zondervan: Submit your review of this book by writing to *zreview@zondervan.com*.

Free Online Resources at
www.zondervan.com

Zondervan AuthorTracker: Be notified whenever your favorite authors publish new books, go on tour, or post an update about what's happening in their lives at www.zondervan.com/authortracker.

Daily Bible Verses and Devotions: Enrich your life with daily Bible verses or devotions that help you start every morning focused on God. Visit www.zondervan.com/newsletters.

Free Email Publications: Sign up for newsletters on Christian living, academic resources, church ministry, fiction, children's resources, and more. Visit www.zondervan.com/newsletters.

Zondervan Bible Search: Find and compare Bible passages in a variety of translations at www.zondervanbiblesearch.com.

Other Benefits: Register yourself to receive online benefits like coupons and special offers, or to participate in research.

ZONDERVAN®

ZONDERVAN.com/
AUTHORTRACKER
follow your favorite authors